LET'S VISIT LIECHTENSTEIN

Let's visit
LIECHTENSTEIN

NOEL CARRICK

ACKNOWLEDGEMENTS

The Author and Publishers are grateful to the following organizations and individuals for permission to reproduce copyright illustrations in this book:

Colorpix Photo Library; Mary Evans Picture Library; Chris Fairclough; The Liechtenstein Government Press and Information Office; The Mansell Collection.

CIP data
Carrick, Noel
   Let's visit Liechtenstein.
   1. Liechtenstein – Social life and customs –
Juvenile literature
   I. Title
   943'.6'48053   DB886

ISBN 0 222 01142 4

Burke Publishing Company Limited
Pegasus House, 116-120 Golden Lane, London EC1Y 0TL, England.
Burke Publishing (Canada) Limited
Registered Office: 20 Queen Street West, Suite 3000, Box 30, Toronto, Canada M5H 1V5.
Burke Publishing Company Inc.
Registered Office: 333 State Street, PO Box 1740, Bridgeport, Connecticut 06601, U.S.A.
Filmset in Baskerville by Graphiti (Hull) Ltd., Hull, England.
Colour reproduction by Swift Graphics (UK) Ltd. Southampton, England.
Printed in Singapore by Tien Wah Press (Pte.) Ltd.

Contents

LIECHTENSTEIN

Ruggell

Schellenberg

Gamprin

Mauren

Eschen

R. Rhine

SWITZERLAND

Planken

Drei Schwestern

Schaan

Vaduz

Triesenberg

Triesen

Steg

Malbun

Balzers

WEST
GERMANY

EAST

FRANCE

SWITZ.

AUSTRIA

ITALY

AUSTRIA

N

0					5 km
0					3 miles

The Fairy-tale Land

Many people see the principality of Liechtenstein as a fairy-tale land. Several facts contribute to this image. It is a tiny speck of land buried in the heart of the European Alps, a land of magnificent and varied scenery, comprising mountains, high forests, alpine pastures, shaded secluded valleys, wild mountain ridges and picturesque villages. Dotted here and there are the remains of castles, signs of the area's tempestuous past—for throughout its long history, intrigue, violence and greed have led to bloodshed and war. Added to this, the Head of State is a handsome prince, the country was once dominated by witchcraft, and many local legends recount evil doings in the dark forests.

But how far this fairy-tale image is from the truth! Liechtenstein is, in fact, a rich, modern, democratic state. Per head of population it is probably the most industrialized nation on earth, and its inhabitants enjoy one of the highest standards of living in the western world.

It is also a most unusual country. It is the only remaining German-speaking monarchy, and the only nation in Europe which bears the name of its royal family. It is one of the smallest nations on earth, covering only 160 square kilometres (61.8 square miles), and has only 26,500 inhabitants. It has no large

7

A picturesque village high up in the mountains—a typical scene which has contributed much to Liechtenstein's image as a fairy-tale land

cities, the major centre of population being Vaduz, the capital, with about 5,000 inhabitants. Liechtenstein is so small that it does not have many of the things normally associated with an independent nation. It does not have its own currency, but uses the Swiss franc. The principality has no airport, the nearest major one being Kloten Airport at Zurich in Switzerland, 130 kilometres (81 miles) away. Vaduz, the capital, does not even have a railway station. The nearest station is at Schaan, four kilometres (2.5 miles) away. Liechtenstein has no diplomatic representation abroad, except in Switzerland. There is little crime, and unemployment is virtually non-existent. There is no army and, as there are no airfields, it is not possible to have an air force. In addition, as the country is landlocked, there is no need for a navy.

Sandwiched between Switzerland and Austria, Liechtenstein lies on the eastern bank of the upper reaches of the River Rhine, Europe's most important waterway. This flat area of the Rhine's plain comprises forty per cent of Liechtenstein's total area. Although most of this part of the country is completely flat, a strange hill, called the Eschnerberg, juts up out of this flat terrain to a height of 730 metres (2,395 feet). As we shall see, this hill has played an important role in the region's history.

A stone marking the southern boundary of Liechtenstein, one of the smallest nations on earth

Looking south across the River Rhine towards Switzerland, Liechtenstein's western neighbour

Beyond this flat area, much of the country is mountainous, with a steep slope of the Alps, known as the Drei Schwestern mountains, extending westwards from Austria. The highest point in Liechtenstein is a mountain called Grauspitz, which is 2,599 metres (8,527 feet) above sea level. Even the lowest point in the country, near the village of Ruggell in the far north, is 433 metres (1,421 feet) above sea level.

Geologically, Liechtenstein is a fascinating area. It is the point where two huge mountain ranges—the Western and Eastern Alps—meet; and the boundary between these ranges runs more or less from north to south, passing through Liechtenstein's capital, Vaduz. Millions of years ago, however, the area was covered by sea. Today, the nearest sea is the Adriatic at Venice, 300 kilometres (188 miles) away, but evidence of the ancient sea can be seen high up in Liechtenstein's mountainous region. This is because some prehistoric volcanic eruption cast up the ancient sea bed; and fossilized shells, fish teeth, shellfish, reef limestone, sea urchins and even seaweed can still be found today.

Despite its alpine situation—which makes it an important centre for downhill skiing—Liechtenstein's climate is relatively mild. High in the Alps, temperatures may fall as low as minus

Fossilized shells, discovered at a point which is now far above sea level

15 degrees Celsius (5 degrees Fahrenheit) in winter. But in summer, temperatures range between 20 and 28 degrees Celsius (68 and 82 Fahrenheit).

Although Liechtenstein is an industrialized nation, it has no slums or areas of noticeably poor housing—or even extensive industrial areas. The industrial plants are widely scattered and are mainly carefully planned to blend into the surrounding countryside. Once an impoverished, neglected pawn in international power politics, Liechtenstein is now a politically stable, prosperous and internationally-renowned state, thanks mainly to the economic and social transformations of the last three decades.

Man has transformed Liechtenstein, not merely by creating new industries but also by eliminating some of the natural hazards inherent in living in an alpine region. Over the centuries, the Rhine changed its course and flooded frequently, making permanent habitation of the land near its banks hazardous. As late as 1927, massive floods devastated much of the valley and only in recent times have banks sufficient to keep the river in check been constructed.

Development during the twentieth century has enabled Liechtenstein to emerge as a proud, politically independent nation with its own institutions, flag, national anthem and culture.

The flag of Liechtenstein consists of two horizontal bands of equal width, blue above and red below, with a prince's golden crown in the top corner. Because of Liechtenstein's lack of formal contacts in many countries (it has no diplomatic representation abroad, except in Switzerland, and belongs to few world organizations in its own right), this flag is not widely recognized.

Strangely, no one really knows the origins of Liechtenstein's national anthem, although the words are believed to have been written in the mid-nineteenth century by a German pastor who lived in Balzers. The anthem has five verses, and is sung to the same tune as the British national anthem, *God Save the Queen.* It is sung in German, but an English translation of the first verse is as follows:

> *On the banks of the young Rhine*
> *Lies Liechtenstein, resting*
> *On alpine heights.*
> *This beloved homeland,*
> *Our dear fatherland,*
> *Was by God's wise hand*
> *Chosen for us.*

Despite recent attempts to improve Liechtenstein's image abroad, the principality still remains one of Europe's least known nations. Several years ago, a survey carried out in the United Kingdom revealed that nearly half of those questioned had no idea, not only of where Liechtenstein was, but that there was even a nation of that name. Things are rapidly improving as the country's cultural and business connections and its flourishing postage stamp trade reinforce the principality's position as a true nation in every sense of the word.

13

The People and their Language

Liechtenstein has a population density of 165 persons per square kilometre (422 per square mile). This is somewhat higher than the average population density of the twelve nations of the European Community, which is 142 persons per square kilometre (367 per square mile). The population is distributed unevenly over the eleven communes of Liechtenstein, with Vaduz, the most densely populated commune, having about 5,000 inhabitants. Tiny Planken, which has an area of only five and a half square kilometres (just over two square miles), is the least populated commune, with less than three hundred people.

Symbol

The Liechtenstein coat of arms—a symbol of the nation's independence

Vaduz, Liechtenstein's capital and its most densely populated commune, with about five thousand inhabitants

As we shall see when we examine their political and other institutions, Liechtensteiners are a mixture of conservative and modern. The Liechtenstein written constitution is probably the most up-to-date, clearest and best written constitution of any nation in the world. It is held up as an example of how a modern democratic constitutional monarchy should work. Yet, at the same time, conservative views persist. It is only since 1984 that women have been allowed to vote on national issues—and women are still not allowed to vote on local issues in several parts of the country.

15

Liechtensteiners keep traditional values in many other ways and put into practice what many other nations only claim to uphold. For example, Liechtensteiners belive in peace and, to illustrate this, have abolished their army. Cynics might say that it would be impossible for a nation the size of Liechtenstein to defend itself anyway. The last Liechtenstein army was abolished in 1868 and its last soldier died in peaceful old age in 1939, at the age of ninety-five.

The fact that Liechtenstein has managed to keep out of all wars in the twentieth century has had an effect on the outlook and personality of the people. This peaceful approach also manifests itself in politics. There are only two major political parties, nicknamed the Reds and the Blacks; and they have been in a more or less trouble-free coalition since 1938.

Liechtensteiners are fiercely proud of their differences from the peoples of surrounding nations and passionately defend their right to their independence. This does not mean, however, that they are closed to foreign influences. One person in three in Liechtenstein is a foreigner. (Out of a total population of 26,380 in 1982, 9,590—or 36.3 per cent—were foreigners.) One of the burning political issues in the principality is *Überfremdung,* which can be translated roughly as ''too many foreigners''. The use of this term does not mean that Liechtensteiners do not like foreigners—because they all realize that the principality and its industry need them. It means simply that some Liechtensteiners are worried that the presence of so many people from outside may dilute the strong local cultural heritage or that there may be permanent divisions in Liechtenstein society. Liechtensteiners would like to see the foreigners integrating more closely with local people and adopting their cultural outlook. In addition to the foreigners actually living in Liechtenstein, about one-quarter of the country's workforce crosses the border daily from Austria and Switzerland to work in the factories, banks and company offices. The influx of foreigners is likely to remain a concern for many years to come.

The fact that Liechtensteiners are so intensely proud of what they are may explain why the process of a foreigner becoming a citizen of Liechtenstein is so complex. An applicant for citizenship does not go first to the central government, but to the commune where he or she resides. All citizens of that commune have the right to attend a meeting where they vote on whether or not they want the applicant to become a citizen.

Schaanwald Customs post on the border between Liechtenstein and Austria. Thousands of tourists pass through this point every year

If they agree, the applicant is then sent to the central government. The Diet—the nation's parliament—then votes to give its approval. Then, if the Diet approves, the application goes to the Prince—and it is he who has the final say.

Liechtensteiners tend to be a law-abiding people. The nation has only forty-two policemen who belong to an organization with the resounding title of The Princely Liechtenstein Security Corps. One of the reasons why there are so few police is that, apart from Liechtensteiners being very law-abiding, there are fewer routine police tasks to perform. For example, the small area of the country means that there are few roads to patrol, and less guard and security patrol work.

To help the full-time policemen on special occasions, however, there is an additional group of thirty men who act as an auxiliary police force. These are men with normal jobs who don uniforms and help the regular policemen when there is a big state function or when they are needed to control traffic or if there is a large-scale man-hunt or mountain rescue operation.

Liechtenstein's policemen are trained in Switzerland. They wear splendid uniforms comprising an olive green jacket and trousers, a green shirt and a flat peaked cap. The police work in very close co-operation with such voluntary organizations as alpine patrols and the Red Cross, as well as with the police forces of Switzerland and Austria.

Article Six of the Liechtenstein constitution states simply: "The German language is the national and official language". While everybody speaks and reads standard German—and all official documents are in this language—most Liechtensteiners, when speaking among their friends, speak a dialect of German called Alemannic. This dialect varies both in pronunciation and sometimes even in meaning from area to area. The dialect goes back many centuries to the Germanic tribe called the Alemanni, who settled in some parts of the Rhine valley not long after the end of Roman domination of the area. At the time, the local people spoke Latin and Rhaeto-Romance, which was a corruption of Latin and local languages. It is thought that these two languages were spoken side by side until around the tenth century when the Germanic tongue of the Alemanni became the predominant one. In one area, another dialect called Walser is in common use. This is in the Commune of Triesenberg. In the thirteenth century, people from the Swiss canton of Valais settled there and they have maintained their own language ever since. However, there are no linguistic problems in Liechtenstein and all citizens can freely converse with each other. In this respect, Liechtenstein contrasts sharply with neighbouring Switzerland where many people are unable to communicate with people from different parts of the country because they speak different languages.

History

THE ANCIENT PEOPLE OF THE MOUNTAINS
Man has inhabited the region that is now Liechtenstein for about 5,000 years, since the Middle Stone Age. In those days, the valleys of pleasant green meadows and tranquil rivers and streams which we know today did not exist. The River Rhine, which today flows calmly between well-defined banks, then had an irregular course, ever changing and constantly flooding. This made it impossible for early man to farm the same fields continuously or to build permanent habitations on the river plain. Even without the vagaries of the Rhine, farming was difficult. At this time, the flat parts of the country consisted largely of bog and large areas of gravel beds, along which the river waters flowed from time to time, or of dense brushwood. In addition, freak, sudden rushes of water frequently crashed down the courses of mountain streams, bringing down rocks, dirt, trees and other debris onto the valley floor. These natural hazards continued to make life very difficult for the inhabitants of the valley until the nineteenth century.

Nevertheless, communities were established. Important prehistoric settlements have been discovered at Malanser and Schneller, and the many artefacts found there tell us much about the early inhabitants' way of life and skills. Despite the problems

The River Rhine, shrouded in mist. Many centuries ago, the river changed course frequently, making it difficult to establish permanent settlements in the area

which they faced, they seem to have been relatively advanced, living by growing crops on what fertile scraps of land they could find and by breeding cattle. They did not live on the floor of the valley but retreated every evening to their settlements, which were almost certainly fortified, on Gutenberg and Eschnerberg hills.

Who were these early Liechtensteiners? They seem to have been members of a powerful and warlike Alpine tribe known as the Rhaetians. Little is known of the history of the Rhaetians. One theory is that they were of Etruscan origin; and this seems to be borne out by the fact that small stone figures of soldiers, discovered near Balzers, have helmets very like those known

Gutenberg Castle. It was to elevated areas such as this that the early inhabitants of the region would retreat each evening

to have been worn by the Etruscans in Italy. By this period, shortly before the start of the Christian era, it seems that the land was in the possession of Celtic tribes who had amalgamated so completely with the original inhabitants that, generally speaking, the Rhaetians may be regarded as a Celtic people.

22

Strong Celtic influence can be seen even today in many of modern Liechtenstein's place names.

In about 15 B.C., the Romans arrived in the region. By this time, the inhabitants of the valleys had developed a structured society, with an organized religion in which they made sacrifices to their gods. The area very quickly became important to the Romans who, at this period, were steadily expanding their enormous empire.

Two Roman generals, Drusus and Tiberius, both stepsons of the first Roman emperor, Augustus, conquered the local Rhaetian people; and the area became part of the Roman province of Rhaetia. Augustus himself had ordered a road to be built through the area, enabling the Romans to reach the Splügen and Julier passes and thus cross over the high Alps. As the years passed, the Romans built many fortifications to protect the road—a major one being at Schaan, a modern Liechtenstein commune.

The Romans had a lasting influence on the area and introduced, among other things, the cultivation of the vine and wine-making, and the Christian religion. They also introduced the Latin language and, as in many places occupied by the Romans, the local inhabitants gradually began to speak a language which was a mixture of Latin and their old local language.

After the Romans left in the fifth century A.D., the history of Rhaetia became more complicated. Germanic tribes had gradually penetrated into most of the surrounding lands and

Augustus, the first Roman emperor, who ordered a road to be built across the high Alps

a people called the Alemanni settled in some parts of the region. Like most parts of central Europe, the area that is now Liechtenstein eventually became part of the Holy Roman Empire under the emperor Charlemagne.

Charlemagne, who was born near the present Belgian city of Liège in A.D. 742, extended his dominion over much of the former Roman Empire in Europe. When the Holy Roman Empire was divided on Charlemagne's death (because his grandsons could not agree over who should become king of the entire empire), Liechtenstein became part of the territory owned by the Counts of Bregenz, who were related to Charlemagne by marriage.

24

However, these territories where later divided again and again. Any real connection with the modern country of Liechtenstein does not emerge until 1342, when the County of Vaduz, which includes much of the upper part of modern Liechtenstein, was created. The intrigue, greed, bargaining and fighting which occurred—which was typical of what was happening in this period over most of Europe—culminated when a nobleman with the high-sounding name of Count Hartmann III of Werdenberg-Sargans-Vaduz moved into the Castle of Vaduz. Ever since then, the castle has been the residence of the local ruler or his representative.

UNIFICATION

In 1396, the County of Vaduz became part of the developing Austrian Empire, owing allegiance to King Wenceslas. Another important date in Liechtenstein's history is 1434, when the northern part of present-day Liechtenstein, which belonged to noblemen called the Lords of Schellenberg, also became part of the Austrian Empire and was joined to the County of Vaduz. Thus the two parts of modern Liechtenstein, the County of Vaduz, now known as the Upper County, and the area of the Lordship of Schellenberg, now known as the Lower County, became one.

However, unification did not bring peace. Local people did have some say in their affairs by electing certain officials, but this influence had little bearing on the politics of the region as a whole. During the fifteenth century, three wars were fought over the area and, during the last war, in 1499, the Castle of Vaduz was burned down.

Just ten years later, the County of Vaduz and the Lordship of Schellenberg were sold to another noble family, the Counts of Sulz. This sale had two important and lasting results. Firstly, Count Rudolf of Sulz, the first member of the Sulz family to own the region, linked his land closely with Austria. In a treaty with the Austrian emperor Maximilian, Rudolf agreed that the newly reconstructed Vaduz Castle should always be open to Austrian troops. Secondly, Count Rudolf prevented the Reformation taking hold. Until the sixteenth century, all

The Red House in Vaduz, which dates from the time when the County of Vaduz and the Lordship of Schellenberg were combined under the rule of the Lords of Schellenberg

Christians in western Europe were Roman Catholics. The Reformation was a movement which aimed to reform certain aspects of the Catholic Church. It led to a split within the Church and, ultimately, to the birth of Protestantism. Because of Rudolf's action, Liechtenstein remains to this day predominantly Catholic.

The Counts of Sulz ruled for just over a century. While this was not a period of prosperity, it was at least a period of peace. The last of the Counts of Sulz, Count Charles Ludwig, gave his subjects political and other rights and ruled fairly by the standards of the era. He was, however, beset by problems— the principal one being lack of money. He had inherited great debts from his brother and, to pay some of them, in 1613 he sold the County of Vaduz and the Lordship of Schellenberg to yet another noble family, the Counts of Hohenems. Disaster followed almost immediately. Eight years later, a war between Austria and several areas of Switzerland led to troops being quartered there for fifteen years. In 1647, a Swedish army threatened to invade but only came to the frontier. The payment to the Swedes of a huge ransom prevented them from looting and plundering. As if that was not enough, the bubonic plague—known as the Black Death—swept through the country soon after the wars, and a large percentage of the population died. Most of the remainder fled the flat country into the alpine regions in an effort to escape the plague. Then followed a wave of witch-hunts of an intensity unparalleled anywhere else in the world. This was to be the darkest period in the area's history.

An engraving of the trial of a witch. Although witch-hunts were commonplace throughout Europe, they were particularly intense in the area which is now Liechtenstein

LIECHTENSTEIN BECOMES LIECHTENSTEIN

Until this moment in history, the area was not actually called Liechtenstein. The country received its name from the next noble family to buy the County of Vaduz and the Lordship of Schellenberg. The sale came about for the time-honoured reason—the owning family ran short of money.

The Counts of Hohenems had ruled so badly that the emperor of Austria appointed a high official to go there and see what could be done to help the nation. The official, who was both a prince and an abbot, deposed the Count of Hohenems and, in an attempt to clear up some of the unhappy Count's enormous debts, sought buyers for the County of Vaduz and the Lordship of Schellenberg. First to go under the hammer was the Lordship of Schellenberg. It was bought by an Austrian nobleman, Prince Hans Adam of Liechtenstein. Thus in 1699, the House of Liechtenstein, based near Vienna, came into the history of the area.

The Prince did not buy Schellenberg to help its people. His motive was somewhat less noble. In Vienna, there was an Assembly of Princes. People qualified for membership of the Assembly by holding a territory under the dominion of the Austrian Emperor. Prince Hans Adam desperately wanted the power and prestige that came with membership of the Assembly. He was a rich man—known at the time as ''Hans Adam the Rich''—and he acquired Schellenberg solely to qualify for membership. He paid 115,000 florins for the area. This was not enough to pay off the debts of the previous ruler so, in 1712, Hans Adam the Rich bought the County of Vaduz as well. Five years later, the County and the Lordship were officially united and proclaimed to form the Imperial Principality of Liechtenstein—the only country in Europe which bears the name of its ruling family to this very day.

At first, the Liechtenstein family displayed little interest or affection for the poverty-stricken country which bore their name. Many of its people remained serfs long after that system had been abolished in other parts of the Austrian Empire, and it was many years before the Princes of Liechtenstein so much as set foot in the country.

The next major change in Liechtenstein's constitution occurred in 1806, when Napoleon created the Confederation of the Rhine. This was a group of sixteen small states, including Liechtenstein, which came under French authority. Napoleon granted each state sovereign status—and so, although under French protection, Liechtenstein became for the first time a sovereign state. Despite this, the then Prince of Liechtenstein, Prince John I, remained in the Austrian army and fought against Napoleon.

At the Congress of Vienna, which took place after Napoleon's final defeat at Waterloo in 1815, Liechtenstein joined the thirty-nine states of the German Confederation. It remained a member until the confederation was disbanded in 1866, the year war broke out between Prussia and Austria.

The break-up of the confederation meant that, for the first time, Liechtenstein was a fully independent nation, owing no allegiance to any other power, confederacy or grouping.

It seems incredible that although the Princes of Liechtenstein had owned part or all of what is now Liechtenstein since 1699, not one of them had ever visited the principality. Even Prince John I, who ruled from 1805 to 1836 and was responsible for many political and social reforms, never set foot in his dominion. The first Prince of Liechtenstein to actually set foot in this country was Prince Aloysius II, who visited it in 1842—143 years after his family had acquired the principality. And none of the princes lived permanently in the principality until

Prince Franz Josef II came to the throne in 1938 and established his home in Vaduz Castle.

Despite the lack of interest shown by the House of Liechtenstein until comparatively recently in the country's history, their ownership led to one fact that was of enormous benefit to the people. As a sovereign nation, Liechtenstein was able to assert its independence from all the major powers of Western Europe. It was thus able to avoid being dragged into both the First and the Second World Wars and is, therefore, one of the few parts of western Europe not to have experienced war on its soil in the nineteenth and twentieth centuries.

Government

Liechtenstein is a constitutional monarchy. This means that the monarch—in this case, the Prince of Liechtenstein—rules, as in Britain, with the help of an elected parliament. The parliament is called the *Landtag,* or "Land Diet", and comprises fifteen members elected every four years. The rules by which both the Prince and the Diet operate are laid down in a written constitution. The tiny size of the Diet makes it even smaller than local municipal councils in most other countries.

As well as having a central government, the principality is divided administratively into two halves, both of which are further divided into communes. In the half known as the Oberland, or Upper County, are the communes of Vaduz, Balzers, Planken, Schaan, Triesen and Triesenberg. In the Unterland, or Lower County, are the communes of Eschen, Gamprin, Mauren, Ruggell and Schellenberg.

One factor makes Liechtenstein somewhat less democratic than other democracies of western Europe. Women are not allowed to vote in elections for some of the communes and were granted the vote for the Diet only recently, following a referendum (in which only men could vote) held in 1984. However, although women are now allowed to vote on national issues, many Liechtensteiners are not in favour of this. (This

32

A general view of the commune of Triesenberg in the Upper County

can be seen in the extremely narrow margin by which women were granted the right to vote—51.3 per cent of voters in the referendum were in favour, while 48.7 per cent were against.) Switzerland is the only other European democracy which places such restrictions on the rights of its women citizens.

The way the Liechtenstein government functions differs in many respects from the governments of larger democracies such as the United States of America or Great Britain. The greatest

The Government Palace in Vaduz. Liechtenstein's parliament, with only fifteen members, is smaller than many municipal councils in other countries. The prime minister is a civil servant

difference is that the prime minister is a civil servant and is not an elected member of the Diet. The prime minister is assisted by four government councillors. The prime minister and the four councillors are all nominated by the members of the Diet, and their appointment is made by agreement between the Diet and the Prince. One of the councillors is nominated as deputy prime minister. While the posts of prime minister and deputy prime minister are full-time, the other three councillors serve only on a part-time basis, and usually have some other job.

34

The prime minister has very great influence and, in fact, supervises most of the business before the government. The prime minister and the Prince must both sign any bill passed by the Diet before it can become law. However, although the prime minister and the councillors are responsible for the administration of the principality, they do come under the control of the Diet.

Liechtenstein uses the proportional representation system to elect the fifteen members of the Diet. This means that any candidate who receives at least eight per cent of the national vote is guaranteed a seat in the Diet. After each election, the oldest elected member of the Diet organizes a vote to select the Diet's president and vice-president who will direct the parliament's affairs for the whole of its four-year term. Each member of the Diet must swear allegiance to the Prince, to uphold the constitution and to promote the welfare of the country to the best of his ability.

Another way in which the Liechtenstein parliament differs from those of Britain and the U.S.A. is that bills put before the Diet can come from three sources. Bills can be introduced by a member of the Diet, or by the Prince or, under a constitutional right which brings democracy down to the level of the people, by the citizens themselves. This is done in one of two ways. If a petition is signed by six hundred citizens, or if a resolution is passed by three of the eleven communes at communal assemblies requesting a bill, then the Diet must debate it. And the constitution states that such bills must be debated in the next sitting of the Diet. There is no way in which the Diet can avoid facing any bill it does not like.

Both the Prince and the people can also force the dissolution of parliament. The Prince may do so whenever he likes, but an election for a new Diet must be held within three months. The people can dismiss parliament if a petition is presented by nine hundred citizens or if a resolution is passed by four communes at communal assemblies requesting dissolution.

Generally speaking, the Diet operates with lively debate but not too much serious wrangling. This is because the nation's only two parties have governed in coalition since 1938.

The two parties are the Progressive Citizens' Party, known popularly as the Blacks, and the Fatherland or Patriotic Union, known as the Reds. Both parties are conservative, both base their ideals on Christian principles, and both have the same motto: "Faith in God, Prince and Fatherland". Although foreigners can see little basic difference between these two parties, Liechtensteiners insist that there are differences and that this means that the principality is not, therefore, just a one-party state.

As well as debating laws, parliament nominates all judges and magistrates who are then officially appointed by the Prince. In fact, Austrian and Swiss judges are accepted in Liechtenstein, as Liechtenstein law is based, in general terms, on the laws of Switzerland and Austria. Most criminal and civil laws are based on those of Austria, while company law is based on the Swiss model.

36

While talking about the way Liechtenstein is ruled, mention must be made of the role played by the eleven communes. Apart from their power to introduce legislation in the national Diet, or to dismiss it in extreme cases, the communes run their own local police forces, allocate money for schools, promote cultural pursuits, levy rates or local taxes and perform many other functions carried out by local government everywhere.

The Monarchy

In keeping with the image which many people have of Liechtenstein as a fairy-tale kingdom, the nation is ruled by a handsome prince. Liechtenstein is the only European country which is named after its royal family, and the Liechtenstein family, as distinct from the nation of Liechtenstein, is one of Europe's oldest noble families.

The first written record of the family name dates from the first half of the twelfth century, when one Sir Hugo of Liechtenstein is recorded as being the owner of Liechtenstein Castle, situated near the town of Modling near Vienna. One famous Liechtenstein, Henry I, is known to have led the Austrian army to victory against invading Hungarian forces at about the time William the Conqueror was changing the course of English history. Thus the House of Liechtenstein is historically as ancient as any in Europe.

By the end of the Thirty Years War, the Liechtenstein family was one of the richest and most distinguished in the Austro-Hungarian Empire. Two family members, Charles I and Rudolph II, occupied the highest positions, being respectively Governor of Moravia and Lord High Chancellor of the Imperial Court in Prague, which was then part of the Empire. Charles I later became Governor of Bohemia and, being an extremely rich man, was able to lend the Emperor money to continue a war against invading Turkish armies which were threatening the very existence of the Empire. For this, the Emperor elevated Charles to the rank of prince in 1608.

However, it was another three generations before the House of Liechtenstein became associated with the territory which is now called Liechtenstein. If the present Crown Prince is counted as a ruler, thirteen princes have sat on the Liechtenstein throne in uninterrupted succession.

It is largely the work of the monarchy that has transformed Liechtenstein from being a poor farming community into a highly industrialized nation with a higher per capita income than Switzerland, its prosperous neighbour to the west. The person mainly responsible for this is Prince Franz Josef II. He has twelve other Christian names (Maria, Alois, Alfred, Karl, Johannes, Heinrich, Michael, Georg, Ignatius, Benediktus, Gerhardus, Majella), and is the only monarch in history to be a fully qualified forestry expert.

When Prince Franz Josef II came to the throne in 1938, he was almost immediately confronted with the most serious problems which the principality had faced in centuries. The German Third Reich, under Adolf Hitler, threatened hostilities against the defenceless little nation. It was through the Prince's determination and the fact that Liechtensteiners affirmed that they were a totally separate nation from Austria, owing total allegiance to the Prince, that the principality avoided being dragged into the Second World War. After the war, Prince

Prince Franz Josef II, who came to the throne in 1938, not long before the outbreak of the Second World War

Franz Josef directed his energies towards improving Liechtenstein's economic position, and was very successful.

The present situation of the monarchy is a little confusing. In 1984, although he did not abdicate, Prince Franz Josef named his eldest son, Crown Prince Hans Adam, as his deputy, and passed over to him the reins of office. By coincidence, the new ruler bears the same name as the prince who first became associated with the nation of Liechtenstein.

Prince Hans Adam, a trained economist, was born in 1945 and became the first member of the Liechtenstein royal family to go to school in the principality, attending a normal primary school in Vaduz. He later went to other schools in Vienna and then in Switzerland. He graduated in economics from the School

40

of Economics and Social Sciences in St. Gallen, Switzerland, and also worked for a period for a bank in London.

According to Liechtenstein's constitution, the monarch is the Head of State and his person is sacred and inviolable. His powers and duties are very clearly defined in the constitution. He has, in theory, some absolute powers. For example, he can dismiss the parliament, but elections in which he plays no part must be held within twelve weeks of parliament's dismissal. He may enter treaties with foreign countries, although these are not valid unless approved by parliament. However, he acts independently of the parliament in ensuring the administration of the law. He may even pardon criminals and shorten their sentences.

The Prince retains the ancient right to confer titles, orders,

**Crown Prince
Hans Adam
of Liechtenstein**

awards and decorations on those who have served the nation well, and decides who shall receive which award. Today, the ancient titles of nobility, such as Baron and Count, are seldom conferred. However, various orders of chivalry, such as the Order of Merit, are awarded. The Order of Merit comprises a number of grades, including such titles as the Commander's Cross with Star of the Liechtenstein Order of Merit, the Grand Cross with Diamonds of the Liechtenstein Order of Merit, and the top-ranking award, the Grand Star of the Liechtenstein Order of Merit.

Because of Liechtenstein's tiny size, there is no doubt that the Prince of Liechtenstein is closer to his subjects than any other of today's monarchs. The Prince knows a large proportion of his subjects personally, and is held in high affection. The

Prince Franz Josef II, on a state visit to Austria in 1984. The Prince is largely responsible for Liechtenstein's prosperity

enthusiasm with which important birthdays are celebrated is evidence of this. The emphasis of the monarchy in Liechtenstein has changed remarkably over the last half-century. In the past, the monarchs were Austrian princes devoting some of their time and energy to the tiny area which bears their family name. They also had other territories which engaged much of their attention. Today, this has changed and the principality is their sole interest.

Agriculture and Industry

A visitor to Liechtenstein, seeing the farms, orchards, green fields, vineyards and forests, could well be excused for thinking that he was in a sleepy, rural, agricultural land. What he does not always realize is that hidden behind this rural exterior are the factories and workshops which make Liechtenstein, on a population basis, the most highly industrialized nation of Europe. Liechtenstein's industrial workers happily escape the dreariness that characterizes industrial areas in many other nations. Factories are often located in the most pleasant surroundings, enabling workers to enjoy all the advantages of a peaceful rural life with the added security of having a regular job and salary.

This is not to say that agriculture is not important. However, the number of Liechtensteiners working in agriculture has dropped enormously since the Second World War and now comprises only three per cent of the working population. The small area of land available is, of course, a major reason why agriculture employs so few people. The nation's total area of 16,008 hectares (39,556 acres) comprises 2,982 hectares (7,369 acres) of pastoral land and meadows; 912 hectares (2,254 acres) of open arable land; 2,514 hectares (6,212 acres) of alpine pastures, where livestock can graze in summer, but not in

Sheep grazing on lush pasture in the south of Liechtenstein

winter; 5,560 hectares (13,739 acres) of forests; and 4,040 hectares (9,983 acres) of built-up areas and wasteland.

Agriculture is assisted by the relatively mild climate of the Rhine valley, which is largely the result of a warm, dry wind from the south, called the Föhn. The Föhn warms the earth and the air, making it possible for vegetation seldom found so far north to flourish. When this mild climate is combined with a high rainfall—between 1,000 and 1,200 millimetres (39 and 47 inches) per year—conditions for a high yield of crops are virtually guaranteed.

About one quarter of the agricultural land is used to raise crops, the principal ones being maize and other fodder for cattle. Vegetables grow well on the alluvial soil low in the Rhine valley.

A typical Liechtenstein farmhouse. Thanks to the relatively mild climate (due to the Föhn) and high rainfall, Liechtenstein's farms produce high yields of crops

So well do they grow that there is a processing plant in the main vegetable-growing area in the Schaan commune; and Liechtenstein exports such canned vegetables as spinach, beans, peas and carrots.

An unusual product for a nation as mountainous as Liechtenstein is wine. It is only thanks to the Föhn that grapes are able to ripen in Liechtenstein—otherwise it would be far too cold. The wine-growing area is small, comprising only about 15 hectares (37 acres). Wine production varies between 60,000 and 90,000 litres (13,200 and 19,800 gallons) per year. Most of the wine is produced by small, family-owned vineyards and is of the red Burgundy type.

Both beef and dairy cattle are raised in Liechtenstein, the

46

cattle being the famous brown animals common in Austria and Switzerland. Traditionally, cows and calves were driven each spring to graze on the lush growth of the alpine pastures and then driven down again as winter approached. This practice was widespread until the 1950s, but the number of cattle taken to the high country is now declining, despite government efforts to keep the tradition going.

In addition to cattle, sheep and pigs are also raised. However, sheep are mainly bred by part-time ''hobby'' farmers as a sideline to their main occupation, which is usually working for one of the industrial organizations. There were once many goats, but nowadays they play no significant role in agriculture.

Blended into the rural scenery are the manufacturing and other

Tucked away behind the trees is one of Liechtenstein's small factories. Many factories are attractively landscaped to blend into the surrounding countryside

industries—Liechtenstein's main economic assets. About 5,500 people work in these industries and in trade and building. This is somewhat less than half the total workforce of just over twelve thousand. The workforce also includes over five thousand resident foreign workers and almost four thousand workers who cross the frontier from their homes in Switzerland or Austria each day to work in Liechtenstein.

Although there were companies manufacturing products in Liechtenstein a century ago, Liechtenstein in those days was a poverty-stricken enclave where the standard of living was generally very low. The population was involved almost exclusively in rural pursuits, and most people lived very miserably on whatever they could grow. Liechtenstein's industrial revolution has occurred mainly since the Second World War. The success of the drive to industrialize can be seen in the fact that such a high percentage of the workforce is today employed in secondary industry—that is, in plants making finished or semi-finished products. This percentage is much higher than West Germany, commonly regarded as Europe's most efficient industrialized nation, where only forty-three per cent of the workforce is employed in industry.

Two things characterize Liechtenstein's industry. Firstly, because the principality has few natural resources, all raw materials are imported. Secondly, no major industrial centre was ever created. The result of this is that even quite large industrial plants are situated in predominantly rural areas.

Because Liechtenstein's domestic market is so small, industry could not survive unless most of the products manufactured there were exported. The business-like Liechtenstein manufacturers know that high technology products sell best—they have established many highly sophisticated industries to make such goods.

The major industries are metal-working, engineering, textiles, instrument-making, ceramics, chemicals, pharmaceuticals, and food products. Some of the industries are unusual, but nonetheless very profitable. For example, the principality is one of the world's major producers of false teeth and other dental products. Its dentures and other dental products are exported to ninety countries. However, other exports go mainly to the twelve nations of the European Economic Community.

The strength and sophistication of manufacturing industry makes a major contribution to the very high standard of living which most Liechtensteiners enjoy. Although the nation was affected by the economic problems of the late 1970s and early 1980s, it fared much better than many of its neighbours. Its unemployment rate at no time rose above one per cent of the working population—a remarkable achievement.

In general, commercial operations in Liechtenstein are small. There are 1,300 registered commercial enterprises. These range from tiny one-man farms to large manufacturing concerns and banks with international operations—although, on average, each has only twenty employees. Liechtensteiners believe that the small average size of commercial operations reflects their love of independence.

The Ivoclar factory in Schaan, which makes false teeth and other dental products—one of Liechtenstein's more unusual industries

It is not possible to talk about Liechtenstein's commercial life without discussing tourism. There is one very odd fact about tourism in this nation—no one has any idea of the number of tourists who visit the principality each year! The reason is very simple: the vast majority of tourists enter Liechtenstein, stay for a few hours, and then leave again without staying overnight. As there is no check on the border between Liechtenstein and Switzerland, those entering are not counted. We do know that some 175,000 tourists stay overnight in the principality each year. Liechtenstein is the only nation in the world which can claim that well over seven times as many people visit it each year as live there. If a nation such as France had this ratio of tourists to residents, it would have something like 350,000,000 tourists a year. Most tourists come from Germany and Switzerland, but many come from further afield—notably the U.S.A., Britain, France and the Low Countries. Tourism is expected to increase when an Art Centre, designed to house the Prince's world-famous art collection, is built.

Those in the tourist business are confident that their industry will continue to grow. They are anxious to attract even more tourists. *"Liechtenstein—go to it, not through it"* is their slogan.

Commerce and Banking

Liechtenstein is a land of often bizarre statistics. One of the strangest is that there are probably two companies registered in the principality for every person living there. This is because Liechtenstein is best known in the business world as a "tax haven". There are many such tax havens around the world. The phrase "tax haven" simply means that companies which register their headquarters in such a place pay much less tax than if they were registered in a larger country. Many of these companies use Liechtenstein simply as a letter-box. A company is registered there but conducts all its business abroad. How does this happen? There is simply an address to which the company's mail is sent—to prove that it is registered there—and the mail is then sent on to the country in which the company really operates.

Why is Liechtenstein regarded more highly than many other tax havens? This is a complex question, but part of the answer lies in the fact that Liechtenstein's currency is the Swiss franc, which is one of the strongest currencies in the world. (This means that it usually holds its value against other currencies.) The principality is also in the Swiss economic zone and shares the Swiss reputation for economic strength, honesty and reliability. In addition, Liechtenstein is socially and politically very stable.

People establishing companies there know that they do not risk losing their assets by sudden changes in law, government or currency levels.

Liechtenstein is also a member of an organization called EFTA, or the European Free Trade Agreement. This came about when Switzerland joined EFTA and allowed Liechtenstein, because it shared the same currency and had the same Customs regulations, to join at the same time. Later Switzerland, and thus Liechtenstein, signed a free trade agreement with the European Economic Community. Thus foreign companies setting up business in Liechtenstein have access to markets in the twelve nations of the E.E.C.

Other reasons for Liechtenstein's popularity are that taxes are extremely low, even when compared with other tax havens, and that the country's company laws—which govern how a company may operate—are less stringent. There is also complete fiscal security, which means that neither Liechtenstein's government nor any individual may disclose the assets or liabilities of companies registered there. So tight is this fiscal security that it is not even possible to ascertain the actual number of companies registered there. Experts who study Liechtenstein as a tax haven estimate that there are at least 40,000 "letter-box" companies—in a country with a population of just over 26,000.

However, Liechtenstein is careful that the wrong kinds of business do not take advantage of its liberal company laws. In other words, it takes steps to ensure that it keeps out criminals

53

or anybody else whose business dealings may not be above board. There are a number of highly complicated checks designed to stop people abusing the laws. Some ''letter-box'' companies were involved in a number of financial scandals in the mid-1970s, during which large sums of money were improperly channelled. The laws were changed to prevent this happening again and, as a result, several companies moved their headquarters to other tax havens where they felt they would be able to operate more freely.

One Liechtenstein law expressly forbids any company registered there from harming the principality's reputation abroad by its business dealings. This gives the Liechtenstein government wide powers of control.

The presence of ''letter-box'' companies benefits Liechtenstein in two ways. Firstly, even the low taxes imposed on ''letter-box'' companies provide about one-third of the nation's income. Secondly, these companies are known to employ nearly one thousand people, which is a considerable percentage of Liechtenstein's workforce.

Contrary to the popular belief that Liechtenstein is a banking centre comparable to Switzerland or Luxembourg, there are only three banks in the principality. They can all be regarded as Swiss banks in many ways, because all are members of the Swiss Bankers' Association and have agreed to observe most of the rules of this association. The most important aspect of this is absolute secrecy. Liechtenstein banks claim that the penalties for breaking their secrecy regulations are much more severe than those in Switzerland. The only place where bank secrecy can be waived is in a court of law in which very serious criminal charges are being decided.

The principality is such a small place that there are only limited possibilities for investing money in Liechtenstein industry and commerce. Thus much money from Liechtenstein is channelled through Swiss banks to investment opportunities in Switzerland and other countries. Vaduz is not a banking centre in the sense that the cities of Zurich or Luxembourg are banking centres. However, the very stability of the Liechtenstein political and economic situation ensures that its banks are trusted and regarded as secure and stable places in which to deposit money.

Vaduz, the Capital

Vaduz, the capital of Liechtenstein, is a beautiful place. Although it is the capital of an independent nation it is a small village rather than a town or city, and has a population of only about 5,000 people. The village nestles under the castle, which is surrounded by vineyards. In summer, when the green leaves are lit by bright sunshine, it is a lovely sight. The scene is no less beautiful in autumn, when the vine leaves turn golden. Vaduz is a historic place and is first mentioned in records dating back to 1150. The very beauty of the village, with the castle dominating it, fits in well with Liechtenstein's romantic image. Many tourists visit the principality for only a few hours at the most and often take away little more than an impression of Vaduz and its stately castle. But Vaduz deserves more than a quick glance. Far from being a mere romantic-looking spot, it is industrialized, modern, wealthy and sophisticated. It is a commercial centre, the seat of government of the nation and, at the same time, the major centre of population in the country.

Until the economy boomed after the Second World War, Vaduz was a quiet rural place. It had a reputation for producing fine wine and excellent food. It still maintains that reputation, but in addition is now a bustling commercial centre with light industry, well-stocked shops, banks and offices. However,

Vaduz, surrounded by vineyards, nestling under the castle

because it is so captivating, tourism is the principal industry. At the height of the summer tourist season, as many as sixty tourist buses can be seen at any one time in the Staedtle, the town's main thoroughfare.

The principal attraction, and Liechtenstein's most famous building, is Vaduz Castle, home of the ruling prince. The castle was first mentioned in a deed dated 1322, when the area was ruled by the Counts of Werdenberg-Sargans. It was for centuries a kind of political football, frequently changing hands. In 1499, a Swiss army captured it and burned it to the ground. It was soon rebuilt and, by the time the first Count of Liechtenstein

57

gained possession in 1712, the structure as we see it today was virtually complete.

Today, the castle is the private home of the Prince and his family. Visitors cannot appreciate the full beauty and strength of the castle, as it is not open to the public. Some parts of the massive stone wall are five metres (sixteen feet) thick. There are two impressive bastions, at the north-east and south-west corners. The castle was extensively renovated in 1905, and today stands magnificent as a symbol of the solidarity of the tiny nation.

Vaduz Castle, the residence of the Prince of Liechtenstein

The centre of Vaduz—a remarkably quiet capital

Vaduz is one of the few national capitals which visitors can explore fully during a one-day visit. It is unique in its beauty, minute size and cultural treasures. It also avoids that other great problem which bedevils most capital cities—traffic jams. Liechtensteiners consider they are in a traffic jam if they have to wait for a minute or two behind a tourist bus discharging its load of curious passengers!

Education and Culture

Because Liechtenstein is so small, all education comes under central government control. The state school system is divided into kindergarten, primary, secondary and special remedial schools. Until just before the Second World War, young Liechtensteiners had to cross the border into Austria or Switzerland to complete their secondary education. Although some pupils still do this, youngsters are now able to complete their education in their own country. There are both state-run and private schools, although private schools also receive government support. Education in Liechtenstein is not free and parents must pay their children's school costs. In some cases, however, pupils can obtain financial help from the government if their parents cannot afford to pay the full amount. Scholarships are also available.

Since the 1920s, education in Liechtenstein has had close connections with the Swiss education system. Liechtenstein has no university or teacher training college, and most Liechtensteiners who want to pursue their education beyond secondary school study in Swiss establishments.

There are two interesting educational establishments which illustrate the advances that Liechtenstein has made in specialized education. An Evening Technical College was founded in Vaduz

60

in 1961, providing courses in engineering and architecture. Pupils at this college must already have completed a practical apprenticeship course or other occupational training. The second well-known advanced educational establishment is the Liechtenstein Music School, also in Vaduz. This opened in 1963 and has become widely known for its high standard of instruction for both singers and instrumentalists.

Those schools not run by the state are run by the Roman Catholic Church. Most Liechtensteiners (eighty-two per cent of the population) give their religion as Catholic. Seven per cent of the population are Protestant, while the remainder belong to a number of other religions.

Liechtenstein (or Rhaetia, as it was then) was Christianized in the third century A.D. The religion was brought by Christian traders, officials of Imperial Rome, and military personnel who travelled through the area on their way to the far-flung outposts of the Roman Empire.

Catholics far outnumber Protestants because, as we have seen, the Reformation scarcely touched Liechtenstein. Despite the predominance of Catholicism, the constitution guarantees the right of every person to practise his or her own religion freely. The constitution even makes it illegal to differentiate between people because of their religious beliefs. However, the constitution recognizes only the Catholic Church under public law. Thus the Catholic Church is the State Church, and the State guarantees its protection.

A schools complex in the lowlands at Eschen

It is significant that the Catholic Church prints one of the three newspapers which appear in Liechtenstein. This is called *In Cristo* and is published once a fortnight. The other two newspapers are the organs of the principality's political parties. The *Liechtensteiner Volksblatt* (''People's Paper''), published five days a week, gives the views of the Progressive People's Party. The *Liechtensteiner Vaterland* (''Fatherland'') is the voice of the Patriotic Union Party. The *Volksblatt* is the only daily newspaper produced in Liechtenstein itself, being printed in the Commune of Schaan, while the *Vaterland* is printed in Buchs in Switzerland.

Liechtenstein's greatest cultural asset is the Prince of

Liechtenstein's art collection. This is one of the finest private art collections in the world, containing hundreds of masterpieces from many different schools. It is incredible that there exists in a village as tiny as Vaduz an art collection that is the envy of cities and even nations with many thousands of times the population and wealth of Liechtenstein. It is one of the oldest and, second only to that held by the British royal family, largest private art collections in the world, containing not only paintings but sculptures, firearms, armour, silver, porcelain, tapestries and furniture.

The first steps in establishing the fabulous collection were

The parish church of Bendern. Liechtenstein is a predominantly Catholic country but there is complete religious freedom

taken by Charles, the first Prince of Liechtenstein, who lived from 1569 to 1627. He lived in Prague and, for his own pleasure, filled his home with paintings, tapestries, golden objects and ornately inlaid furniture. He passed on his love of beautiful things to his son, Prince Charles Eusebius, who became renowned as a connoisseur of art.

Prince Charles Eusebius is considered to be the real founder of the Liechtenstein art collection. To guide his own son, Prince Charles Eusebius laid down firmly the principles for adding to the collection. He insisted that only the best painters be commissioned to paint special subjects and that only the work of renowned artists be purchased.

One after another, the princes added to the collection. It must be said that the motive of some later princes for purchasing more art treasures was not always a noble one. The possession of an outstanding art collection was proof of dignity, nobility, taste, wealth and, above all, importance. The Liechtenstein family palace in Vienna became a famous gallery, containing a collection second only to that of the Emperor of Austria. A catalogue of works in the collection was first published in 1767 and listed 501 major paintings. By 1873, the catalogue listed 1,451 paintings, as well as hundreds of other precious items. The quality of the works was maintained at the highest level. Almost every famous artist was represented. Even at that time, it was not possible to put a value on the collection, and it is even more difficult to do so today.

Although Princes of Liechtenstein have resided in Vaduz since

1938, the art collection remained in Vienna until the closing stages of the Second World War. The family feared that the collection might be destroyed and, towards the end of the war, transferred it to the safety of neutral Liechtenstein. The art treasures have since been kept in Vaduz Castle, the Prince's residence, which is unfortunately not open to the public.

Parts of the collection are, however, placed on display from time to time; and, in 1980, the Liechtenstein government decided to build a special gallery to house the collection and to display it to the world.

The principality's artistic treasures are not always confined within the nation's borders. Occasionally, works from the Prince's art collection are sent abroad. For instance, the Prince's collection of the works of the Flemish master, Peter Paul Rubens, was on display at the Metropolitan Museum, New York, for many months.

In the main, the Prince's art collection represents the work of people outside Liechtenstein. This is not to say that Liechtensteiners themselves do not display artistic ability. On the contrary, the exhibitions held regularly by the Liechtenstein Artists' Guild have brought much critical acclaim.

In addition to conventional forms of art, some traditional crafts still continue to be practised; but, as in many countries, these are fast dying out and one seldom sees today the skill of former generations in carving clogs, making intricate rakes, basket weaving and coopering (the making of barrels). Modern

Liechtenstein crafts, however—pottery, sculpture and woodcarving—are regarded as the finest in the European Alps, and their fame has spread far beyond Liechtenstein's frontiers.

Liechtenstein has a strong cultural tradition, particularly in the rural areas. For many decades, country districts have had their brass bands, and male and mixed choirs. The tradition of singing extends to operetta; and the principality has two highly esteemed operetta companies, at Vaduz and at Balzers.

Another aspect of a country's culture can be seen in its traditional food. But is it possible for a country as small as Liechtenstein to develop its own distinctive cuisine? Liechtensteiners admit that while there is no widespread national

A *Pietà*, which stands outside the church in Vaduz and is a fine example of modern Liechtenstein art

A wayside crucifix near Schellenberg—an example of the skill of local woodcarvers

cuisine as such, there are several dishes which are certainly peculiar to different parts of the country.

These dishes include *Törkarebl,* which is a cross between porridge and dumpling. It is made by mixing cornflour, milk, water and salt, and boiling the mixture until it turns into a glutinous mass which is then fried in butter. Traditionally, milky coffee is drunk with *Törkarebl.*

Another national dish, fascinating in the way it is cooked if not in its taste, is *Hafaläb.* It takes great patience to prepare it. Firstly, a dough is made by mixing cornflour and wheat-flour with water. This dough is then rolled into small cylindrical loaves which are dropped into boiling, salted water. After a few moments, the loaves rise to the surface. Then they are left for

67

A brass band—always popular in Liechtenstein

hours until they have dried out. They are eaten after being sliced and fried in butter or other fats.

Käsknöfle is yet another Liechtenstein dish. A paste, made from flour, water, eggs, salt, oil and nutmeg, is squeezed through a perforated board to form noodles which are boiled in water for a few seconds. They are then laid in an oven-proof dish with grated cheese, topped with a layer of fried onions and butter, and baked. This dish is served with salad or apple sauce.

68

Sport and Recreation

When one thinks about sport in Liechtenstein, winter snow sports come immediately to mind. Because of its size, the principality has relatively small areas of alpine resorts but, despite this, they are among the most popular in the entire European alpine region. The major downhill ski resorts are at Malbun, 1,600 metres (5,250 feet) above sea level, and Steg, 1,300 metres (4,260 feet) above sea level. These resorts combined have about 20 kilometres (12.5 miles) of downhill slopes. Malbun is the major resort, and has two chairlifts, four ski lifts and two world renowned ski schools. It is also one of the most beautiful ski resorts in the Alps.

In days gone by, the Malbun area had the reputation of being full of ghosts and evil spirits, and none of the inhabitants would remain there over winter. Traditionally, they left the valley just before Christmas when the heavy snows came, abandoning it to the evil spirits until the snows melted in spring. Today, however, the valley is much more densely populated in winter than in summer, as ski enthusiasts flock to the hotels, chalets and private homes which cater for their needs. One attraction is that prices here are not as high as they are in some neighbouring resorts. Another advantage is that recent road improvements ensure that the roads are always passable. Years

A ski run just above Malbun

ago, the roads were sometimes blocked by snow, and skiers were faced with extended stays in the valley—whether they wanted to remain there or not.

The resort of Steg is particularly popular for cross-country skiing and has a beautiful 14-kilometre (9-mile) long cross-country course called the Valuna-Lopp. A 1.7-kilometre (one-mile) stretch of the course is floodlit. The experience of cross country skiing by night is one of the great thrills of this sport. There are other marked ski trails up to 32 kilometres (20 miles) in length.

The mountains also provide great pleasure for walkers in summer. A network of footpaths winds its way through the

70

splendid alpine scenery, leading the walker into high altitude valleys, gentle grassy slopes, steep and wild mountain ridges, and picturesque plateaux bathed in the clearest and purest summer sunlight. Several communes issue maps for hikers, and the Liechtenstein National Tourist Office has published a very useful booklet describing eighty-five different hikes and fifteen mountain walks.

In addition, there are ''educational'' walks which give a fascinating insight into the nation and its people. The most famous of these is the Eschnerberg Historical Mountain Track, in the commune of Schellenberg. The Eschnerberg is a hill which juts out of the Rhine plain. Rising above the marshy terrain of the surrounding low-lying land, it provided a refuge for

A cross-country skiing course in Steg. One of the major centres for this sport, Steg is a popular winter holiday resort

A toboggan run in Steg

prehistoric man. As the walker passes through the woodlands, hills and valleys along the track, a series of notice-boards provides information about the people and events that have, at various times throughout the ages, shaped the area's history. It is like an open-air museum—but most of the exhibits have not changed in centuries.

Most Liechtensteiners are very sports-minded, and over nine thousand of the principality's citizens belong to the National Sports Union. Swimming, tennis, mini-golf (but not golf, as Liechtensteiners say that if the principality had golf courses there would not be enough space for anything else!), bowling and archery are all popular sports. The government is anxious to promote physical education and has established a National

72

Sports Council which provides finance for sports clubs and associations. Liechtenstein takes part in the Olympic Games and other international sporting events and even plays a prominant role in international sports administration. From 1974 to 1980, the chairman of the Liechtenstein National Olympic Committee was a board member of the European National Olympic Committee. Liechtenstein athletes have participated in the Olympic Games since 1936, principally in skiing, tobogganing and athletics.

The great attractions of the outdoor life have ensured that the boy scout and girl guide movements have flourished. There are scout troops in ten of the eleven communes. The scout movement in Liechtenstein dates back to 1927, when the River Rhine flooded, causing extensive damage to large areas of the flat plain country. Volunteers, including scouts, came from neighbouring countries to help repair the damage; and Liechtensteiners were so impressed by the scouts' work that they decided to start their own scout movement. Today there are few major international jamborees which do not have at least one Liechtenstein representative. The girl guide movement exists in nine communes and they too participate in international camps and conferences.

Other major outdoor activities include hunting and fishing. Liechtenstein is divided into nineteen different game reserves. Sections of the reserves are leased to groups—but never to individuals—to ensure that as many people as possible can use them. However, would-be hunters must take a test to prove that

Liechtenstein youngsters enjoying themselves in a swimming pool in Eschen. The government is keen to promote sport of all kinds

they can handle a rifle skilfully before they are granted a hunting licence.

Although wildlife is plentiful, only certain species may be hunted. Ibex, otters, alpine hares, weasel and many kinds of birds, including heron, wild geese and crane are protected by law. Hunters may stalk other game, provided it is not during the breeding season. The range of legal game is very large, considering the limitations of the land area, and includes several types of deer, chamois (goat-like mountain creatures with two huge horns), badger, hares, sanglier (wild boar) and several species of birds, such as ducks and pheasants.

74

Fishing in Liechtenstein is controlled by an act passed in 1869 which proved so effective that only minor changes have been made since. At one time, many of the streams were polluted by industrial waste. The construction of treatment plants, and a law preventing the discharge of waste into rivers and streams have led to an improvement in the quality of water and a consequent rise in the numbers of fish—the most common fish being trout.

Customs and Traditions

Liechtenstein is rich in folklore and its unusual customs and famous legends have made a major contribution to its image as a mysterious mountain land.

Many customs surround Liechtenstein weddings. Perhaps the most widespread is for the bride and groom to emerge from the church to find that their way down the street has been barred by a rope held by village children. The best man comes to the rescue and bribes the children with coins. Weddings seem to be a good excuse for Liechtenstein youngsters to make a few francs. During the feast which traditionally follows a wedding, the bride must be careful that someone does not grab one of her shoes, and make off with it. The shoe is then held to ransom and not returned until the poor best man again pays up. On occasions, the bride herself is "kidnapped", and her new husband must pay his friends to return her.

Another old wedding custom no longer encouraged—in fact, it is now illegal—is to fire off rifles and shotguns into the air. So many people have been injured in the past that periodic attempts are made to stop this practice. But there are few weddings where somebody does not fire the traditional shot— and hastily put away the firearm before a green uniformed policeman appears to investigate.

Perhaps the most colourful traditional ceremony occurs in autumn when the cattle, which have grazed on the alpine meadows over the summer months, are brought back to the lower country for winter. The cow which has given the most milk leads the others down the slope. She is decorated with heavy metal bells around her neck. Small replicas of wooden milking-stools, covered with colourful ribbons are tied to her horns, and her head is covered with silver tinsel. Traditionally, a wooden heart is perched amid the tinsel. It is a great honour for a farmer to have his cow selected to lead the procession down the mountain, and decorated hearts are proudly displayed on barns and stables. Unfortunately, few cows now graze the high country in summer and there are not so many cows and calves in the procession. But the tradition is still maintained.

Another custom takes place on Bonfire Sunday, the first Sunday of Lent. Village lads elect a leader called the "Bonfire Master", who organizes them to collect wood for a huge bonfire. On Bonfire Sunday, the boys walk through the village, and the villagers hand them wood, straw and other inflammable material to add to their fire. When it is dark, the fire is lit and the boys stand in a circle around it, each holding a blazing torch. They form patterns in the air with the torches, the ceremony looking sinister and eerie in the dusk of the evening. Traditionally, the boys troop home when the fire dies down, and their mothers give them a supper of pancakes.

Boys love the bonfire festival. Younger boys enjoy even more a custom which takes place on "Dirty Thursday" or "Sooty

A display of wooden hearts on a barn. A heart is awarded each autumn to the cow chosen to lead the other cattle down from the alpine pastures for the winter

Thursday'', the last Thursday before Lent. On this day, the boys are allowed to gather soot from the chimneys. They then lie in wait for their friends and rub soot in their faces and in their hair. Boys are not the only victims. Girls have soot thrown on them if they venture out—but most remain well behind closed doors on that day. In some parts of the country, on the same day, the boys play another traditional prank. It is the custom that this is the one day of the year when boys can steal a pot of soup from village houses and drink its contents. The idea is to trick the housewife into leaving her kitchen. The soup pot is then stolen and later returned, often with an old shoe inside. However, frequently the boys drink the soup only to find that the housewife has put an old shoe in the pot before it was stolen.

78

In all wine-producing areas, festivals linked with the grape harvest are common—and Liechtenstein is no exception. No one may pick the grapes until a special committee decides that they are just right for harvest. Traditionally, a worker known as the "grapeherd" waits in the vineyard until word from the committee is brought to him. Then he signals the start of the harvest by solemnly ringing the bell in the village church tower.

A major religious event is the feast of Corpus Christi. On this day, there is a procession in which all members of the village take part. People carry devotional objects as they wend their way through the village past their homes, which are decorated with religious pictures, flowers and burning candles.

Witches and Legends

There have been many dark periods in Liechtenstein's history, but none has been less happy than the half century which followed the sale of the County of Vaduz and the Lordship of Schellenberg to the Count of Hohenems in 1613. There were wars, invasions, brutal repression by foreign armies, the plague and starvation. But all these horrors pale into insignificance beside the wave of witch-hunts, the most horific and intense ever recorded anywhere in the world. Witchcraft was part of life in the Middle Ages and its presence was acknowledged all over Christian Europe. As early as 1260, Pope Alexander IV had defined the practices considered as worship of the devil and condemned them. In 1486, two Dominican monks published a guide for authorities on how to conduct a witch-hunt in which nothing was forbidden to force a suspected witch to confess.

Early in the seventeenth century, the population of the region was only about three thousand. Such was the intensity of the witch-hunt that, over a period of thirty years, more than three hundred men and women were arrested, horribly tortured and then executed—often by burning at the stake—for witchcraft.

Witch-hunts were not uncommon in central Europe but why were they so savage and intense in Liechtenstein? No one is really able to explain this, although the fact that the country

A German woodcut depicting witches being burnt at the stake in 1555

was poverty-stricken, its inhabitants primitive and uneducated and its ruler uninterested in his subjects certainly enabled over-zealous authorities to go beyond reasonable limits in applying harsh laws. The country was subjected to a reign of terror which reached its peak about the time of the end of the Thirty Years War in the middle of the century. Many people fled the country, unable to live with the fear that a neighbour would accuse them of witchcraft and that they would be tortured and burned to make them confess. Some of those who fled appealed to the emperor who appointed a special commissioner to investigate.

81

As soon as he arrived, the commissioner stopped the execution of convicted witches, forbade further trials for witchcraft and deposed the Count of Hohenems who had permitted the reign of terror. It was only after the sale of the two areas which make up modern Liechtenstein to the Princes of Liechtenstein that the witch-hunt mania finally died out.

Many of Liechtenstein's classic legends date back to those dark days, for many deal with witches, goblins, giants, dragons and evil and unexplained doings, often in the dark forests. A few examples of shorter legends give us some idea of how witchcraft dominated people's lives at that time.

Once upon a time, a fiddler named Hans Jöri was walking along a road near Balzers in the south of Liechtenstein when he came across a group of well-dressed, obviously rich people. They invited him into a nearby house and offered him food and drink if he would play the fiddle for them. One man told him he could have anything he liked—but when he drank, he must not drink to anyone's health. Hans found himself isolated as the evening wore on and the rich people danced, but he remained on stage and played the fiddle. The hours passed and he forgot the man's warning. He poured himself a drink and, as he was alone on stage, toasted himself: "Cheers, Hans. Your health, Hans. God bless you, Hans," he said to himself. Suddenly, all the well-dressed guests, the food, the drink and even the house disappeared. Hans found himself sitting on the public scaffold in Vaduz, about eight kilometres (five miles) away. He was holding his fiddle in one hand and in the other,

**A sixteenth-century
woodcut of witches
preparing an evil brew. . .**

instead of the silver drinking mug, was the bleeding cloven hoof
of an ox—the symbol of witchcraft. Had Hans played for a party
of witches executed on the gallows? The legend leaves that
question unanswered!

Other legends are very simple, but they illustrate the local
fixation with witchcraft at the time. One is about a farmer at
Schaan who was churning butter. The liquid would not thicken

83

and he suspected that a witch who lived near by was causing the problem. He heated the metal prongs of a pitchfork until they were red hot, and then plunged them into the butter churn. He set to work, and the butter began to thicken immediately. Just then, the witch ran up and asked for butter. ''Why do you want it?'' asked the farmer. ''I have just burned my hands, and I want the butter to soothe them,'' said the witch, holding out her hands to show him. Burned into the flesh were two sear marks, exactly the shape of the prongs of the farmer's pitchfork.

Postage Stamps

Liechtenstein has been called a postage stamp nation—partly because of its tiny size but also because postage stamps are its most famous product. Stamps are so important to this little country that the principality's prime minister is head of a small committee which evaluates all stamp themes and designs. Stamps do many things for Liechtenstein. It is difficult for such a small nation to make its presence felt around the world, but Liechtenstein has a regular method of doing this. Every three months, it produces a new stamp issue which is snapped up by collectors all over the world. Stamps also make sound financial sense, as they provide on average about ten per cent of the nation's income.

Liechtenstein has issued its own stamps since 1912. Before that date, under the terms of a postal treaty between the two countries, Austrian stamps were used. When Liechtenstein's first stamps were issued, Austrian stamps were used alongside them until the end of 1921 when the treaty expired. Liechtenstein then signed a postal treaty with Switzerland. After the signing of this treaty, Swiss stamps were allowed to be used inside Liechtenstein for a short period. The term "forerunner" is used to describe the Austrian stamps used in Liechtenstein before the principality issued its own stamps. All keen collectors distinguish a "forerunner" from an ordinary Austrian stamp of that time by the fact that it carries a Liechtenstein, not an Austrian, postmark. Another term used by collectors of Liechtenstein stamps is "concurrent". This refers to an Austrian or a Swiss stamp issued and used alongside Liechtenstein stamps. These can also be recognized by their Liechtenstein postmark.

Why are Liechtenstein stamps so popular? One reason is that people retain romantic notions about the tiny landlocked principality. Others are more practical in that they hope to make a profit. (Stamp dealers will keep stamps for years, in the hope that they can resell them when their value has risen.) Liechtenstein was the first of the tiny nations to enter the stamp business, and there is more interest in its stamps than in those of other small states. However, a prime reason for the stamps' popularity is Liechtenstein's high reputation in the stamp business. Ever since the production of the first Liechtenstein stamp in 1912, Liechtenstein has taken extreme care not only in stamp production but also in the total honesty of its stamp-trading practices. People know that there is no unfair trading in Liechtenstein stamps and that their lasting value is therefore assured.

The visual appeal also plays a major part in maintaining popularity. This tiny nation is a world leader in the artistic design of postage stamps. The Postage Stamp Design Office in Vaduz is in charge of this. The man largely responsible for setting such high design standards was a former head of this office. Mr. Franz Büchel, who employed young Liechtenstein

Liechtenstein stamps. Liechtenstein is renowned worldwide for both the quality of the stamps it produces and the honesty of its stamp-trading practices. New stamps are issued every three months

artists to design stamps. This policy was continued by his successor, Mr. Hermann Hassler. However, foreign artists are also commissioned to design Liechtenstein stamps. The most famous designers of Liechtenstein stamps are Georg Malin, Louis Yäger, Josef Seger and Hans Peter Gassner.

The motifs on Liechtenstein stamps are varied and cover literally scores of subjects. Naturally, the ruling princes feature prominently, as do Liechtenstein scenes—the most famous one probably being Vaduz Castle. Another source of designs is the Prince's magnificent art collection. Other motifs have included portraits of the leaders of Liechtenstein's eleven parishes, coats of arms, flowers, trees, folklore, religion, historical events, current affairs and special issues to mark certain sporting events. Liechtenstein had an embarrassing moment in 1980 when it prepared a special issue to commemorate the Olympic Games in Moscow. Along with many other nations, Liechtenstein boycotted the Moscow Games and had to destroy the entire issue which it was holding ready to sell.

To date, Liechtenstein has issued more than nine hundred sets of stamps. Most collectors or dealers do not buy separate stamps. They buy whole sets which can contain between three and twelve different stamps. Many are sold directly to subscribers in almost every country of the world.

It is very difficult for even the most expert dealer to predict which stamps will rise most in value. There was one famous case, back in 1934, when what is now Liechtenstein's most famous and most expensive stamp was produced. It was issued to mark the first Liechtenstein National Exhibition in Vaduz and was valid for use for only just over two weeks. It cost then the quite high price of five Swiss francs. The authorities printed 10,000 blocks, but only 7,788 blocks were sold. The remainder, as required by Liechtenstein law, had to be destroyed. One Swiss stamp dealer, known for his sharp eye for a block that might rise in value, refused to buy some blocks at cut price, as he was having trouble selling those blocks for which he had paid full price. Later, he was a very sorry man. Contrary to all predictions, the stamps, which became known as the Vaduz Block, rose steeply in value and now sell for more than 6,000 Swiss francs.

Liechtenstein does not print its own stamps. It employs two famous establishments, the firm of Hélio Courvoisier of La

Chaux-de-Fonds in Switzerland and the Austrian State Printing Office in Vienna. The Hélio Courvoisier company specializes in printing postage stamps and takes orders from scores of countries—not only in Europe but from much further afield. Because its stamps are so popular and speculation on them can be high, Liechtenstein takes care that imperfections in printing do not give them added value. While collectors of most items seek perfection in the things they collect, philatelists (stamp collectors) search for stamps that contain misprints or other faults. To prevent this happening, Liechtenstein stamps are examined sheet by sheet by Swiss post experts in Berne, the Swiss capital city, before they are issued.

To see just how perfect Liechtenstein stamps are, a visit to the Liechtenstein Postal Museum, founded in Vaduz in 1930,

The Postal Museum in Vaduz—its thousands of exhibits are a "must" for anyone interested in stamp collecting

is a "must". On display are all the stamps ever produced for Liechtenstein plus those of Switzerland and Austria which are used in Liechtenstein. In addition, there are thousands of stamps which Liechtenstein has received in exchange for its own stamps from other members of the Universal Postal Union. Samples of artists' designs, sketches and the equipment used to produce stamps can also be seen.

Postage stamps have been described as a nation's visiting-card. Liechtenstein, one of the world's smallest nations, certainly has one of the best known visiting-cards of all. Its famous stamps represent the principality throughout the world.

The Future

What lies ahead for the principality of Liechtenstein and its people? Is it really possible for such a tiny state to continue to remain an independent nation? Liechtensteiners are confident that their country will continue to exist as at present. However, they freely acknowledge that they cannot be totally independent economically, an acknowledgement that stems back to 1852 when Prince Aloysius signed a Customs treaty with Austria. Today, Liechtenstein is in a Customs and economic union with Switzerland and finds the arrangement satisfactory.

A map of the principality of Liechtenstein in the main street of Vaduz. Tiny though it is, Liechtenstein retains its independence and looks forward to a prosperous future

However, the close links with Switzerland do limit Liechtenstein's options in its international relations. For example, Liechtenstein is not a full member of the United Nations, and its policy is not to consider joining until Switzerland does. Although Switzerland has UN agencies on its soil, it is not itself a member. However, Liechtenstein is a member of a surprisingly large number of international organizations. It is a member of some UN agencies such as UNCTAD (Conference on Trade and Development), the Industrial Development Organization, the UN Children's Fund, and the UN Economic Commission for Europe. Other international organizations in which the principality participates include the International Court of Justice, the Universal Postal Union, the International Atomic Energy Agency and the International Telecommunications Union.

Although Liechtenstein has no defence treaties with other nations, it feels as secure as any of the nations which comprise the North Atlantic Treaty Organization (NATO). Liechtenstein knows that any aggression against Western Europe would involve all NATO nations and that, in effect, it is protected by the collective security which NATO provides.

Thus Liechtenstein proceeds into the late twentieth century with a stable economy and its sovereignty as secure as that of any other European nation. Unique in so many respects, tiny Liechtenstein can look out from its alpine stronghold content in the knowledge that it has earned, and can hold, its place among the nations of the world.

Index